D.I.Y.

Do It Yourself

girl

D.I.Y. girl
Do It Yourself

The real girl's guide to making everything from lip gloss to lamps

by Jennifer Bonnell

illustrated by Monica Gesue

PUFFIN BOOKS

PUFFIN BOOKS

Published by the Penguin Group

Penguin Putnam Books for Young Readers,

345 Hudson Street, New York, New York 10014, U.S.A.

Penguin Books Ltd, 80 Strand, London WC2R ORL, England

Penguin Books Australia Ltd, 250 Camberwell Road, Camberwell, Victoria 3124, Australia

Penguin Books Canada Ltd, 10 Alcorn Avenue, Toronto, Ontario, Canada M4V 3B2

Penguin Books (N.Z.) Ltd, 182-190 Wairau Road, Auckland 10, New Zealand

Penguin Books Ltd, Registered Offices: Harmondsworth, Middlesex, England

Published by Puffin Books, a division of Penguin Putnam Books for Young Readers, 2003

10 9 8 7 6 5 4 3 2 1

LIBRARY OF CONGRESS CATALOGING-IN-PUBLICATION DATA

Bonnell, Jennifer, 1975–

D.I.Y. girl : the real girl's guide to making everything from lip gloss to lamps / by Jennifer Bonnell ; with illustrations by Monica Gesue.

p. cm.

Summary: A step-by-step guide to making clothes, beauty products, fashion accessories, and decorative items for the home using commonly available materials.

ISBN 0-14-250048-8

1. Handicraft—Juvenile literature. [1. Handicraft.] I. Gesue, Monica, ill. II. Title.

TT171 .B66 2003 745.5—dc21 2002031800

Printed in the United States of America

Book design by Linda McCarthy with Kristina Duewell and Tony Sahara

Photography by David Mager, Pearson Corporation

To Karen Bonnell, Dorothy "Lady" Bonnell, and Hertha "Oma" Flack Monroe. Three women who embody the D.I.Y. spirit by never being afraid to break the rules and never taking anything too seriously.

Thanks to

Joy Peskin and Kristin Gilson for convincing me to write this book and supplying endless amounts of encouragement during the whole process.

Tracy Tang for saying yes in the first place.

Shannon Dean for all the guidance and patience, not to mention the boundless enthusiasm and willingness to let me cut up her jeans.

Linda McCarthy, Deborah Kaplan, Kristina Duewell, Tony Sahara, Karen Popernik, and everyone else at Puffin and Penguin Putnam for putting the book together and making all look good.

Sharren Bates and Charlie Bonnell for humoring me.

Teresa Kietlinsky for supplying all kinds of support, supplies, and cool ideas.

Aimee Slater and Natasha Heflin for letting me drag them to every craft store in the tristate area and their "offers" to take the finished products off my hands.

Aaron Myerson for coming up with a number of surprisingly good titles. Who knew?

And to my parents, Karen and Tom Bonnell, for letting me borrow (some may say break) the sewing machine over and over, nodding appreciatively at the end results, and never getting angry at my early D.I.Y. adventures—especially the one where I ended up covering the kitchen in salt dough. It was sparkly.

Table of Contents

Introduction

About the Supplies

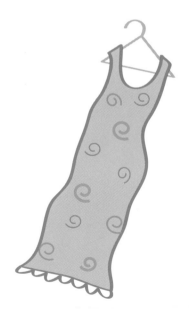

Section 3:   *Decor Diva*

Sources

Introduction

First of all, this isn't your mom's craft book. No super fancy-schmancy boring old home decor, no cheesy fuzzy kittens or sad clowns on sweatshirts. And this certainly isn't your little sister's what-to-do-on-a-rainy-day book. Skip over the string pictures and construction paper. Everything here is easy to make and the end result will have your friends saying, "You made that?!"

Listen, don't get scared off if you don't think you're a crafty kind of girl. Crafty = easily bored + cheap. Because who wants to shell out major bucks for a unique and funky piece when every kid in your high school will have the same unique and funky piece next week? D.I.Y. is all about making cool, original stuff that you like on the cheap. You don't need to be an artist, you don't need to learn how to knit (though it is fun). Anyone can D.I.Y.—it's all in the attitude.

Thanks to a totally crafty mom, I learned a few guidelines of D.I.Y. at an early age:

Follow the directions, but ignore the rules.

Obviously you need to know how to do something, and that's what directions are there for. But where is it written that you have to make something the same size, or the same color, or even remotely the same as the one in the picture? Half the time, the cheesiest crafts have really cool ideas at their core. Follow the directions to learn the procedure, but follow your heart to make something you love.

Nothing is impossible to fix.

Never be afraid to try to make something just because you think you'll screw it up. Made a mistake and think you ruined something? Big whoop. It's not the end of the world. Repaint it, sew it back up, glue it together, cover it with origami paper, or smash it all to bits and stick it in a frame and say it's conceptual art that symbolizes the oppression of creativity and the artist . . . or something.

Don't be afraid to ask for help.

If you don't know how to make something, someone, somewhere out there, does. They'll probably share all their little tips and secrets if you ask them nicely. Don't forget libraries and the Internet. Those babies are godsends when you decide that you really really need to learn how to carve wood at two in the morning. Or is that just me? And hey, if you run into a stumbling block with any of the projects in this book, drop me a line at diygirl@mail.com and I'll help you out.

Perfection is overrated.

Nothing in life is perfect. And I mean nothing. Ignore the little boo-boos and concentrate on the overall picture. Half the time the teeny-tiny mistake that looks glaringly obvious to you isn't at all noticeable to anyone else. And even if other people do notice, they'll probably think it means it was handcrafted especially for some expensive boutique.

Pretty soon you'll be looking at things in stores and thinking to yourself, "Man, I so could make that!" So what are you waiting for, get crafty!

About the Supplies

Almost everything you need to make anything in this book can be found at a craft store (or the craft section of the local superstore like Target or Wal-Mart), health food store, home center, thrift store, or even your grocery store. Can't find what you're looking for? Check out the back for a list of mail order and on-line sources.

Beads and beading supplies:
Craft and superstores have a great selection of beads and beading accessories nowadays, but if you have a local bead shop, definitely check out their selection.

Brushes:
I usually use foam brushes, or cheap, stiff paintbrushes for almost everything. They're dirt cheap and available in craft, home, art, and hardware stores.

Clockwork mechanism:
Craft, art, home, and hardware stores have a variety of clockwork mechanisms, complete with interchangeable hands, for under ten bucks.

Colors for soaps and candles:
A $2.50 package of soap colorants in 3 primary colors found in the craft store or at a soapmaking supply store will last you almost forever. Remember, regular food coloring won't last as long as the dye and may stain your skin. Craft stores and many mail-order soapmaking supply houses also carry candle dyes which can come in powder, solid, or liquid form. Candle dyes aren't meant to go on the skin, so don't make soaps or any other bath product with them.

Decoupage medium:
One of the biggest brand names is Mod Podge®, but every crafting company makes some kind of decoupage medium. Look in craft stores and superstores.

Fabric and batting:
Craft stores and the quilting section of fabric stores are the best places to look for cheap cotton fabric, soft squishy rolls of batting, and pillow forms. Batting comes in rolls (for quilts) and loose (for stuffing pillows and stuffed animals).

Fabric trim, ribbon:
Craft stores have tons of ribbon, but their trim will be expensive. Look at a fabric store's selection of trim instead. It'll probably have more variety and cheaper prices.

Glass jars:
The best and coolest-looking containers come from the dollar store. No luck there? Check out the craft store, hardware store, and even the canning section of the grocery store for pretty jars. Look in your kitchen cabinet for pretty jars and bottles you can wash and reuse—think peanut butter, jam, and even flavorings.

Glass marbles:
These are sometimes called glass nuggets or blobs, and are in the floral decorating section of craft stores, superstores, and home centers. Also check out stained glass supply houses.

Glue:
Really, you only need 3 kinds of glue: a tacky craft glue, a clear multipurpose glue, and a fabric glue. The tacky craft glue should be thick and white and dry clear. Look for Aleene's®, and other brands labeled "all-purpose craft glue." The clear glue has a stronger bond, like Goop® or E6000®. Washable fabric glue will pretty much take care of your every fabric need—just make sure it's permanent and washable. Look in the craft store and hardware store.

Glycerin:
Drugstores and supermarkets carry this thick, clear sticky liquid in the health aisle.

Glycerin soap:
It's available in most craft stores and soapmaking supply stores in 2-pound blocks of clear and opaque white. Look for sales at the craft store and stock up. Check out the local drugstore or dollar store for cheap bars of plain, clear glycerin soap.

Grout:
This is the stuff that goes between tiles and is often found as a white powder you mix with water, but can also be found pre-mixed. Look in home centers and in the mosaic or plaster aisle of the craft store.

Interfacing, fusible or iron-on:
This is white or dark fabric used to stiffen fabric. It has little dots of glue on one side so you iron it onto another piece of fabric and it will stick—permanently. Look for it in craft stores, fabric stores, and superstores.

Lamp shades:
Easy to find and surprisingly cheap in home stores and superstores.

Magnets:
Craft stores, home centers, and hardware stores will all have a good supply of plain magnets.

Paint:
Everything from plain acrylic paint to glass paint can be found at the craft store, the art supply store, or the home center. I tend to go for the kind of acrylic craft paint that comes in small bottles as it's fairly spreadable, easy to clean up with soap and water, dirt cheap, and comes in tons of colors.

Paper, decorated:
I'm a fan of origami paper, which can be found in craft and art stores, as well as a local Asian market. Also look in the scrapbooking aisle of the craft store for non-cheesy designs.

Paraffin and beeswax:
Check in the canning section of the supermarket, hardware store, or health food store for paraffin. Look for beeswax in the health food store. Craft and art stores carry blocks of paraffin, sheets of beeswax, and nuggets of beeswax in the candle aisle.

Rhinestones and studs:
Craft and fabric stores have a good selection of different-color rhinestones and studs.

Scents:
In general, use soap scents for soaps and candles, candle scents for candles only, and essential oils for everything. Candy flavorings are best for lip balms but can be used in anything. Look in craft stores, health food stores, and soap-making supply houses for essential oils, soap scents, candle scents, and candy flavorings. Specialty stores that cater to bakers and confectioners carry an especially wide variety of candy flavorings. Just be careful what kind of essential oils you choose. Some scents can be irritating to skin and aren't appropriate for soaps or lip balms, and others smell yummy but aren't meant to be ingested, so nix the lip balms for those. When in doubt, read the label and ask.

Sealer:
This can also be called water-based varnish or polyurethane and comes in matte, satin (somewhat shiny), and gloss (very shiny) finishes. Check the label to make sure it's water-based and you can clean up with soap and water. I prefer brushing it on from a jar, but it also comes in a spray. Craft, art, home, and hardware stores all have it.

Transfer paper:
This paper transfers images onto T-shirts and comes in either regular or opaque versions. Regular is good for light-colored T-shirts, but you need the rarer opaque for dark T-shirts. Craft stores and superstores usually have the regular version, but check out the office supply stores for both kinds at cheaper prices.

Wicking:
Look in the craft store or hardware store for pre-strung wicking. Or use a flat, cotton-braided string, dipped in melted wax and pulled straight to dry.

Gifty Girl

It's better to give than to receive...but it's fabulous to give something tailor-made!

Decoupage. Fancy word for just gluing stuff down. But hey, it looks cool, it's fun, it's easy, it works on almost anything, and baby, it's calling your name. Decorate boxes, breath-mint tins, picture frames, cars (okay, not cars but you get the idea).

What You Need:

- Paint; acrylic craft paint is best, but any kind will work

- Pictures and words printed from a computer, color photocopied, or ripped from magazines

- Decoupage medium, like Mod Podge®

- Foam brush or other paintbrush

- Water-based varnish or sealer (optional)

- A box, the kind you get jewelry in; or a clean, dry breath-mint tin

If you're decorating a tin or other metal object, you'll also need:

- Gesso (found in art stores and the paint section of craft stores)

How To Do It:

1 If you're decorating a tin, pry open the metal hinges with a metal nail file or screwdriver and remove the lid. Paint the lid with a thin coat of gesso to help the background paint stick to the metal. Let dry.

2 Paint the box or tin with your background color. Use two colors and make a border if you'd like. Go crazy. Let dry.

3 Meanwhile, cut out the images you'd like to use.

4 Use the foam brush to spread a layer of the decoupage medium on the top of the box. Lay your images on top, pressing out any air bubbles or wrinkles with the brush or your finger.

5 While the underlayer is still wet, goop some more medium on top in a thin even layer. Be sure to cover all edges of the images to prevent them from curling up. If you don't want to see any brush strokes, use more decoupage medium and smooth lightly. If you want the box to look all antiquey and textured, press harder and make swirly designs. Let dry.

6 You can keep adding layers of images by following the steps above until you get the design just right.

7 To make the box very durable and very shiny, brush on a coat or two of water-based varnish or sealer. Let dry completely between coats.

TIP Don't have a decoupage medium? Don't worry! Grab some plain white glue, mix with one part water until it's about the consistency of heavy cream, and go to town!

Stick 'Em Up!

MARBLE MAGNETS AND TACKS

So what are you going to put in your decoupaged boxes and tins, you wonder? Why, marble magnets and tacks! The round glass magnifies the mini-images and looks all kinds of classy. These puppies sell for major bucks in stores, but you can crank them out for a few dollars. Beware, these little beauties are addictive and quick to make—good thing they make fab gifts!

What You Need:

• **Flat-backed clear glass marbles**

• **Small images or designs snipped from magazines or printouts from the computer**

• **Clear-drying glue (craft "tacky" glue or thick, clear solvent-based glue both work well)**

• **White paper (optional)**

• **Magnets**

• **Thumbtacks**

• **Small scissors**

Want to package your crafts in style?

Make sets of magnets and package them in decoupaged tins. Package sets of tacks in cork or Styrofoam-lined boxes.

How To Do It:

1 Lay out your images. Leave magazine pages intact and trim the pictures after you've glued the marble on, as it's a little easier to maneuver.

2 Put a dab of glue on the flat side of the marble. Smoosh the marble onto the image (a clear glue really helps here so that you can see exactly what you're doing). Press firmly to get rid of any air bubbles. Glue will come out of the edges of the marble, but be careful not to squeeze too much out, as a thick layer of glue will fill in any imperfections in the marble and give you a nice clear image. Let dry.

3 When the glue is dry, or mostly dry if you're impatient, use small scissors to trim the picture to the marble.

4 If you can see through the image when it's glued, follow the steps above to glue on a white paper backing and trim.

5 Glue the magnet or thumbtack to the back of the marble.

Where are these itty-bitty pictures?

MAGAZINES AND ADS: look for cool abstract designs, those little blobs of color from makeup ads, and tiny pictures in articles.
CATALOGS: check out music clubs, sticker and rubber-stamp stores, toy stores, and museums.
COPY SHOP: take your photos or images and get them color copied and reduced.
COMIC BOOKS: for the cool indie vibe.
ORIGAMI PAPERS: for cool colors and gorgeous, elaborate designs.
WRAPPING PAPER: great for matched sets.
YOUR OWN ART: use markers, paint, stamps, pencils.

A New Spin on Vinyl

HOW EASY? ✄ ✄

So you're all about MP3s. You can't deny that records still look pretty darn cool, and you can pick them up on the cheap at garage sales and thrift stores. Grab a few scratched and warped records with cool labels and covers (don't use Dad's prize classic LP collection!) and make something funky and retro!

What You Need:

- **An old record cover (again, not Dad's. Ask first, or hit the thrift stores!)**

- **Battery-operated clockwork mechanism (available in craft and hobby stores)**

- **An awl or nail**

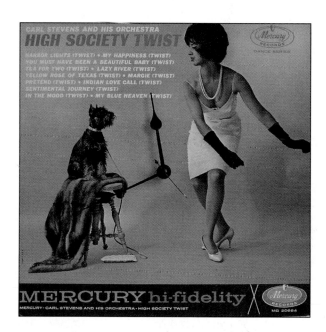

How To Do It:

1 Find the exact center of the cover by connecting the opposite corners on the back. Using an awl or a nail, punch a hole in the cover. Twist the awl or nail around to expand the hole to fit the size of the clockwork mechanism.

2 Push the shaft of the clockwork back through the hole and follow the directions on the mechanism package to assemble the hands.

3 Hang it up! The clockwork mechanism comes complete with a hanger; all you need is a nail.

Rock 'n' Bowl

Now that you've used the album cover, what're you going to do with that record? How 'bout making a cool little wavy bowl for servin' candy at your next shindig? The bowls also make hip planters for your rockin' ferns and daisies.

What You Need:

- **An old record with a cool-looking label**

- **An ovenproof pan or dish**
  (think metal or Pyrex® , not plastic)

- **A cookie sheet**

- **Oven mitts**

- **An oven**

- **Clear, thick glue (optional)**

How To Do It:

1 Turn the oven to 200°F, or low. Put the ovenproof pan or dish upside down on the cookie sheet and place in the oven.

2 Wipe the record clean, and put it on top of the pan in the oven. The heat of the oven will soften the vinyl of the record so that it will start to drape over the side of the pan. This will only take a minute or so, so crack the oven door and don't even think of walking away!

3 When the record is soft, put on the oven mitts and carefully slide the cookie sheet out so you can take the record off the pan and out of the oven. The record will be very hot and very soft.

4 Moving quickly, shape the folds of the record the way you'd like, centering the label on the bottom. If you like, use another upside-down pan to help guide the shape of the record. Let cool.

5 If you want to plug the hole, swipe a small dab of clear glue in the hole and let dry.

TIP The vinyl will cool down and become hard very quickly, so work fast. If it hardens before you are done, pop it back in the oven for a few seconds and try again.

Hello Dolly

HOW EASY? ✂ ✂ ✂

So you've outgrown that old doll. But you've still got her around, right? You can still put it to good use, keep the memories of the good ol' days of second grade alive, AND have a cool and kitchy jewelry box, complete with ring holders! After all, what better use for an old Barbie than a jewelry box befitting her extravagant lifestyle?

What You Need:

- **Old jewelry box, or other medium-size box with lid**

- **Acrylic paint in your choice of color(s)**

- **2 sheets 8½" x 11" decorated paper or 6 sheets origami paper**

- **1 fashion doll (like Barbie™ or one of her friends), or fashion doll parts (arms and head)**

- **Shoes, clothes, hairbrush, comb, or other doll accessories**

- **Decoupage medium or white glue mixed with water**

- **Foam brush or other paintbrush**

- **Strong, clear-drying glue or glue gun**

- **Scissors**

- **Water-based varnish or sealer (optional)**

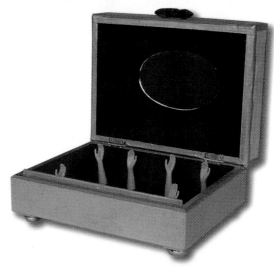

1 Paint the entire inside of the box, and the outside of the bottom half. Let dry and apply a second coat if the old color of the box is showing through.

2 Cover the top half of the box with the sheets of paper using decoupage medium (or glue mixture). Use the foam brush to spread a thick layer on the top of the box and center one sheet of paper over it. Smooth the paper out using your fingers, the brush, or the back of a spoon to eliminate any air bubbles. Snip the overhanging paper at the corners on the diagonal. Coat the sides of the lid with decoupage medium and fold the edges down onto the sides of the lid, overlapping the corners, and smooth. Cut strips from the second piece of paper to fit the sides and fold under the lip of the box. Brush on more decoupage medium. Smooth the paper on and fold under. Let dry.

3 If you like, outline the edges of the box top with paint. Let dry.

4 To make the box very durable and very shiny, brush on a coat or two of water-based varnish or sealer. Let dry completely between coats.

5 Now comes the fun part. Pop the head off the doll and use the scissors to cut the arms off below the elbow. (Feels good, don't it?) Paint the accessories to coordinate, if you like.

6 Use the glue gun or strong glue to glue the head to the center of the lid. Arrange the accessories on the lid and glue them down. Glue a pair of shoes to the front of the lid (above the catch, if there is one). Glue the severed hands inside the box, pointing up, as ring holders. Let dry.

Feel like jazzing up your box?

While the box shown has a top covered with one type of patterned paper, you can decoupage the top with several different images ripped from magazines, toy catalogs, or pictures printed out from your computer. Go to the local copy shop and get cool origami paper or a magazine picture enlarged and repeated in tiles on the color copier. Copiers can also copy in just one or two colors, so that somewhat icky brown paper can turn into sassy little yellow patterns with one touch of the button.

Hot Pots

HOW EASY? ✂ ✂

Your BFF totally digs poetry or your sis is all about the lyrics to some random British band? Make them the perfect gift: a flowerpot with their favorite poem or song written on it. It's super easy and looks very chic even if you don't have the best handwriting.

What You Need:

- **A plastic flowerpot**

- **Acrylic craft paint in a cool color**

- **Foam brush**

- **Paint pen in a contrasting color**

- **A poem or song lyrics**

- **Water-based sealer or varnish (optional)**

How To Do It:

1 Using the foam brush, paint the entire flowerpot with the craft paint. Let dry. You may need to give the pot two coats if the color shows through.

2 Using the paint pen, and starting at the top of the outside lip of the pot, write your poem or lyrics in a spiral down the side. It's easiest to hold the pot in one hand and turn it as you write. Script looks nice and flowy, but you can always print. Try to write fairly large, so the words are readable.

3 If you make a mistake, "erase" it with a little background paint and keep going. When the paint is dry, fill in the mistake.

4 Let dry, and if you like, seal with water-based sealer or varnish and a foam brush.

TIP

If you're having a problem keeping a steady hand, take a deep breath before you start and slowly exhale as you're writing. Or ask someone who's not a spaz to help you.

Don't forget to sign your masterpiece at the bottom!

Don't like the spiral?

Try writing in different designs. Turn the pot on its side and write from left to right so the text runs vertically. This technique works really well on cheap and ugly picture frames, too.

Roses are red.
Violets are blue.
Sugar is sweet.
and so are you!

Glamorous Glass

HOW EASY? ✂ ✂

Etched or sandblasted glass looks cool and frosty, but personalized frosted glass costs a ton and do you really want to deal with acid and a sandblaster to make a candleholder? Use translucent glass paint to get the Pottery Barn look the cheap and easy way.

What You Need:

- **Glass jar, candleholder, or vase**

- **Translucent white glass paint, like Gallery Glass®**

- **A brush**

- **Masking tape**

How To Do It:

1 Decide whether you want to freehand your design or use the masking tape to tape out a design on the jar. Write your BFF's name, or lay out stripes, or just do spirally swirls. Remember that wherever you put tape, the glass will remain clear.

2 Squeeze out a little paint onto a paper plate or a piece of paper. Dab your brush in the paint and then paint the jar with a thin coat. Dab the paint on instead of using long brush strokes to get the most "frosted" look.

3 Let dry, then carefully peel the tape off. If you make a mistake, you can use a metal nail file or your fingernail to peel the paint off and try again.

TIP Be careful when washing your newly frosted jar as the paint is not dishwasher safe. You can also use glass paint that needs to be baked in the oven (follow the manufacturer's baking directions) for a more permanent design.

Keepin' It Under Wraps

BROWN-PAPER GIFT WRAP

HOW EASY? please, not even ✂

Sure you can wrap your gifts in the comics pages, but that's like so third grade. Use silver or gold paint and the brown paper bags from the grocery store and go all Martha-Stewart-via-the-dollar-store on your friends.

What You Need:

- **Brown paper bags from the grocery store**

- **Silver, gold, or other metallic-colored craft paint**

- **Foam brush**

- **Stamps, kitchen sponges, or plastic wrap**

How To Do It:

1 Cut the bags down the seam and cut out the bottom. Unfold, printed side down. If the bag is still pretty creased, you can iron it flat on a very low setting on a smooth, heat-resistant surface, but I hardly ever bother.

2 Now, go to town! Use foam "decor" stamps from the craft store, rubber stamps, kitchen sponges cut to shape, or potatoes cut into cool shapes to stamp your bag with the metallic paint. It's often easier and neater to paint onto the stamp rather than dipping it into a puddle of paint. Put the stamps very close together to make an allover pattern.

Or, using the foam brush, make stripes of different widths and colors.

Or, squish up a handful of plastic wrap, dip in paint, and smoosh over the bag.

3 Let dry, and use clear packing tape to wrap!

Kiss Me, You Fool

HOW EASY? ✂ ✂

Lip balm and gloss. They're yummy, addictive, and come in those cute little containers. But who wants to drop a load of cash on a couple of pots of Mega-Mango goo—and what goes in that stuff anyway? How about making some personalized peppermint lip balm or gloss in an adorable mini-mint tin? It's easy! It only takes about half an hour to make a whole bunch of gifts for all your friends!

What You Need:

- **¼ cup of vegetable, olive, or sweet almond oil**

- **¼ ounce or 1 teaspoon of beeswax, chopped into small pieces or grated**

- **4–5 drops of essential oil of peppermint (or other essential oil)**

- **Heat-safe disposable plastic cup or a clean, microwave-safe glass jar**

- **Disposable spoon**

- **6 empty, clean, dry mini-mint tins or old lip balm pots**

Optional:

- **⅛ teaspoon glycerin**

- **1 vitamin E capsule**

- **Lipstick**

- **Superfine glitter (food-grade)**

Make the base:

1 Pour the oil into the plastic cup or glass measuring cup and add the beeswax. Microwave the oil and wax for about one minute, stirring every 20 seconds, until the wax is completely melted. (Watch out, the cup will be hot.)

2 Test the consistency of the base. Do you want a glossy gloss base that's soft like Vaseline™, or a creamy lip balm base that's a little harder, like Chap Stick™? Dip the plastic spoon in melted base mixture and let the excess drip off. Put the spoon on a small piece of aluminum foil or wax paper and stick it in the freezer for about a minute until it cools. If it's too hard, or you want an even glossier finish, add some more oil, a little bit at a time. If the mixture is too soft, or you want something more lip-balmy, add a tiny bit of wax and stir until it remelts.

Make it fancy:

1 Add the peppermint oil (or other essential oil) and stir well.

2 Stir in the glycerin. You don't have to use it, but glycerin adds moisture and makes the lip balm or gloss smooth and silky.

3 Pierce a vitamin E capsule with a pin and pour the contents into the melted oil and wax. Vitamin E is a moisturizer and helps preserve the final product.

4 Take a small chunk of your favorite color of lipstick and add it to the melted oil and wax mixture. The lipstick won't add a lot of color to your lips, but it will make the gloss look nice.

5 If you want to really sparkle, add a pinch of superfine glitter (make sure it's food-grade) to the mixture.

TIP If your lip base hardens, pop it back into the microwave for about 15 seconds. If it is still too hard, keep microwaving it in 5-second increments until it's totally melted.

Make it cool:

1 When you're all done tinkering, pour the mixture into the tins or jars. If you're using mint tins, check to see if there are holes by the hinges. Be sure the mixture only comes up to the holes or it will pour out. If you're using an old lip balm pot, be careful not to fill the pot all the way to the top.

2 Let mixture cool undisturbed for a smooth professional finish. After about 20 minutes, your lip balm and lip gloss will be ready!

3 If you want to make a label, make up a cool name for your lip balm like "Glittertastic, by Gigi." Cut out a piece of paper slightly smaller than the tin or pot and write the name of your new lip balm on it. Use a glue stick to attach the label.

Mix up the flavor!

Sure, peppermint's great and all that, but what if you're just not a minty kind of girl? How 'bout:

PINK LEMONADE GLOSS= gloss base + lemon oil + chunk of pink lipstick + dash of superfine glitter

ORANGE CREAMSICLE LIP BALM= lip balm base + orange oil + vanilla oil + piece of orangy lipstick

LAVENDER FIELDS LIP BALM= lip balm base + lavender oil + plum lipstick

CINNAMON CLOVE GLOSS= gloss base + clove oil (only use a drop or two) + dash of cinnamon + brownish lipstick

Smack!
Right in the kisser!

Good, Clean Fun!

Soap looks impressive, but it is easy to make. And it's pretty and funky and useful. But you know what the best part is? Easy cleanup.

BASIC SOAP

HOW EASY? ✂ ✂

What You Need:

- **Approximately 15 ounces of glycerin soap, clear or opaque**

- **Soap dyes or food coloring**

- **Essential oils and add-ins (see page 23)**

- **A microwave-safe measuring cup or double boiler**

- **16-ounce dishwasher-safe food container (this is your mold)**

- **Petroleum jelly**

- **Knife**

- **Spoon**

> Check in supplies and sources sections for more details about where to find all this stuff.

How To Do It:

1 Spread a thin layer of petroleum jelly on the inside of the food container (a.k.a. the mold), and make sure to get the bottom and the corners well coated. Use a dishwasher-safe food container as the mold to be sure it can take the high heat of the melted soap.

2 Cut the soap into chunks with a knife, and put them in the microwave-safe measuring cup and microwave in 20-second intervals until melted. If you don't have a microwave, put the chunks in the top of a double boiler, put water in the bottom, and heat over low heat until the soap is melted. Be careful, the soap will be hot.

3 Carefully stir the soap with a spoon and add in a few drops of color and essential oils. Stir in any other fun stuff (see page 23). Pour slowly into the food container mold.

4 Let cool completely, and unmold. Push down on the bottom of the mold to help it along.

5 Slice into bar-sized shapes with the knife.

21

Add-ins:

- **CINNAMON:** Ground cinnamon adds a warm smell and brown speckles to soap.

- **CITRUS ZEST:** Use a zester or a vegetable peeler to scrape away the colored skin of lemons, oranges, and limes and add to your soap for color and scent.

- **COCOA:** Cocoa makes a yummy-smelling and chocolaty brown soap.

- **COCOA BUTTER:** It's super moisturizing and adds a chocolate smell.

- **HONEY:** Honey adds a pretty color and smell to soap, but may make the soap softer and slightly harder to unmold.

- **MILK:** Powdered milk is good for all skin types and will make a clear soap opaque.

- **OATMEAL:** Oatmeal is moisturizing and exfoliating. Grind regular (not instant!) oatmeal in a blender or a food processor and add to the liquid soap.

- **PAPRIKA:** This spice adds color and interesting red speckles.

- **SALT:** Kosher or sea salt looks cool and crystally in soap.

- **SUGAR:** Sugar makes the soap lather better.

- **SUPERFINE GLITTER:** Oooh, shiny. (Check the label and make sure it's food-grade glitter.)

- **TEA:** Use loose tea or open a few tea bags and stir in. Green tea adds an especially nice fragrance.

- **VITAMIN E OIL:** The oil adds moisture and acts as a natural preservative. Pierce a few capsules of vitamin E oil and squeeze into melted soap.

- **WHEAT GERM:** It's exfoliating and homey-looking. Stir well before pouring to keep from settling out.

Molds—they're everywhere!

Craft stores sell special soap molds, but you can find tons around the house, too.

TRY USING:

- **Pringles™ cans**
- **PVC pipe, with one end sealed, using several layers of plastic wrap and a rubber band**
- **Dishwasher-safe food containers (they can take the heat of the soap), preferably disposable ones**
- **Clean, dry paper milk cartons, pint-size and quart-size**
- **Shaped ice-cube trays**

PICTURE SOAP

Embed laminated pictures, playing cards, or cool images in your clear soap.

- Swipe a rectangular mold with petroleum jelly and melt clear soap according to the basic soap recipe. Use a light-colored dye and stir before pouring to thicken the soap.

- To embed the picture on the top of the soap, pour a thin layer of soap into the mold, let cool a minute until it forms a slight skin on the surface, and gently push the image facedown into the soap. Let harden, then pour the rest of the soap into the mold. Cool, unmold, and cut to shape.

- To float the picture in the middle of the bar, fill the mold halfway and let the soap harden. Gently lay the image you want to embed on top of the soap, being careful not to trap air bubbles underneath. Slowly and carefully pour the rest of the soap over the picture. You may need to poke the image down with a chopstick or a fork while the soap is still liquid.

- Let cool, unmold, and trim.

- Melt clear and opaque soap in separate containers, according to the basic soap recipe, and use any mold.

- Color the two batches different, but complementary, colors and stir in a warm, earthy fragrance like vanilla or sandalwood. Stir, to cool the soap.

- Pour the two soaps into the same mold, letting them swirl together. Let cool and unmold.

- Use a knife to cut into bars, then trim into gemlike shapes. Cut off sharp corners on an angle to make facets.

> **TIP** Clean up by hand, and don't use the dishwasher. The soap can lather and cause the dishwasher to flood and leak. Needless to say, the parentals will not be happy if that happens.
>
> Even if your mold turns out funny-looking soaps, trim your soaps to the shape you want. Leftover soap trimmings can always be remelted.

Try These:

LEMON POPPY SEED SOAP: opaque glycerin soap + lemon zest + poppy seeds

TEA SOAP: clear glycerin soap + tea leaves + vanilla extract

OILY-SKIN SOAP: clear or opaque glycerin soap + lavender essential oil + ground oatmeal + calamine lotion

BAKERY SOAP: opaque glycerin soap + cocoa + wheat germ + vanilla extract + cinnamon in which to roll final bars

Bathing Beauties

BATH SALTS

They look pretty. They smell nice. They're expensive as all get out. Glycerin or oil helps keep the salt from drying the skin too much, and powdered milk is fab for oily or dry skin. Oatmeal sounds icky, but does wonders for your skin. Tea leaves are pretty and contain antioxidants. Try them all!

What You Need:

- **1 cup kosher salt**

- **1 cup Epsom salts**

- **½ cup powdered nonfat milk; ½ cup regular oatmeal, ground in a blender; and/or 2 tablespoons tea leaves (optional)**

- **1 tablespoon glycerin or 1 tablespoon vegetable or olive oil (optional)**

- **Food coloring**

- **Perfume, essential oils, or soap scent**

- **Glass jar with tight-fitting lid or stopper**

> **Decorate the jar with frosty paint etching (see page 16).**

How To Do It:

1 In a bowl, mix the salts with a spoon or your hands.

2 Add in any dry additives, like milk or oatmeal.

3 Drizzle the glycerin or oil, and mix with your hands to get rid of the clumps.

4 Color the salts with a few drops of regular food coloring.

5 Mix in a few drops of essential oil or liquid soap scent, or spritz a few times with your favorite perfume.

6 Pour into a glass jar and shake every few days to prevent clumping.

7 Pour about ¼ cup of salts into a running bath for a fab soak!

For the Spiciest Girl You Know

Fancy-pants bath and body shops sell their scrubs and salts for tons of cash, and half the time they only have one icky-smelling flavor. Who needs that? Just raid the kitchen for some salt, oil, herbs, and spices to make your own.

What You Need:

- **1 cup kosher salt**

- **¾ to 1½ cups sweet almond, soybean, walnut, olive, or vegetable oil**

- **3–5 drops essential oil, like peppermint or lemon (optional)**

- **1 tablespoon cinnamon, rosemary leaves, ginger, or other dried herbs; lemon or orange zest (optional)**

- **1 widemouthed glass jar or other container with a tight-fitting lid**

How To Do It:

1 Pour one cup of salt into the glass jar. Adjust the amount until the jar is about half full of salt.

2 Pour in the oil and stir. Add or subtract oil and salt until you get the consistency that you want.

3 Add stuff in. Make it smell yummy and add a couple of drops of your favorite essential oil. Mix in some herbs and spices, like rosemary, lavender, cinnamon, ginger, or citrus zest.

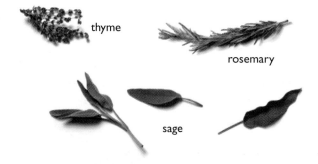

thyme

rosemary

sage

How to use it:

Use in the shower. Step away from the water and take a scoop of scrub out. Rub on dry and rough spots, especially your elbows, knees, and feet, and avoid your face. Rinse. (The oil can make the shower slippery, so be careful.) And remember, as the old saying goes, don't rub salt into an open wound!

Need a whiff? Try these:

Try using peppermint essential oil, lemon zest, ginger, and rosemary for a good wake-up scrub; a mix of cinnamon and ginger for a warm, soothing scrub; or lemon, vanilla essential oil, and (noninstant) oatmeal for a bakery scrub.

Come On, Baby, Light My Fire

Come on now, who doesn't like burning things? OK, OK, so maybe I'm the only borderline pyro running around, but everyone likes candles. They're just so expensive, and sometimes the ones that smell good are plain ugly. So go ahead, grab some wax and make some waxy prezzies for your friends!

BEESWAX CANDLES

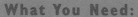

(HOW EASY? ✂)

What You Need:

• **Several sheets of beeswax, less for a thin taper, more for a thick candle**

• **1 cotton wick**

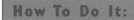

How To Do It:

1 Lay a sheet of beeswax down. Place the wick at one end of the sheet, lining up one end even with the side of the sheet.

2 Roll the beeswax sheet around the wick. Don't press too hard or the wax will crack and your candle will be all lumpy. Make sure to keep the bottom end of the candle even.

3 When you come to the end of a sheet, butt a second sheet onto the end and keep rolling. Use a few sheets for a thin taper or just keep on going to make a nice, fat Pottery Barn–worthy candle.

MOLDED CANDLES

HOW EASY? ✂ ✂ ✂

What You Need:

- 1-pound block of paraffin

- 1 or 2 crayons, or candle dye

- A wick, a few inches taller than your mold

- Clean and dry 1-quart paper milk carton as a mold

- A stick or wooden spoon (that you don't mind ruining)

- Pencil, pen, or handle of said wooden spoon

- Vegetable oil or oil spray as a mold release

- Saucepan

- Coffee can or other disposable metal can with no holes

- Oven mitt or pot holders

- Newspapers

- Candy or wax thermometer

TIP Always melt more wax than you think you'll need to fill the mold or container. You can always let the excess cool and use it again for layered candles. It's a lot harder, and more annoying, to pour half a candle, run out of wax, and then try to match the color again.

How To Do It:

1 Cover your work surface with newspapers. Lots of 'em.

2 Break the paraffin into chunks and place in the coffee can with the thermometer. Pour about 2" of water into the pan and set the coffee can into the pan. Heat on the stove on low until the paraffin is completely melted. Do not let the water boil away; do not let the wax reach over 140°F; and do not take your eyes off the wax even for a minute.

3 Peel the paper off the crayons and break them into the wax. Or drop in a chunk of candle dye. Stir occasionally with the stick or wooden spoon.

4 While the wax is melting, cut the top of the milk carton off and smear or spray a little veggie oil on the interior as a mold release.

5 Dip about an inch of your wick in the melting wax, then put it into the milk carton mold, positioning it on the bottom and holding it in place with the stick or wooden spoon until the wax hardens. Wrap the free end of the wick around the pencil, and rest the pencil on top of the mold, holding the wick taut.

6 When the wax is completely melted, turn off the burner and use the pot holders to take the can out of the water. Be very careful as the pan, the can, and the wax are very hot. Carefully pour the wax into your prepared mold, leaving at least 2" at the top.

Don't pour all of the wax. Let cool slightly, without disturbing, for about an hour.

7 As the wax cools it will shrink away from the sides of the mold and dip slightly around the wick. Remelt the leftover wax as described above and fill the depression, being careful not to go above the original level of wax. Let cool completely. You can put molded candles in the fridge for a little bit to help the cooling process along.

8 When the wax is completely solid, tear away the mold and trim the wick to about ¼".

Fun variations:

- Make scented candles by adding an essential oil or other oil-based scent. Try soap scents, candle scents, and strong-smelling candy flavorings.
- Layered candles are super easy. Just pour one color partway into the mold or container and let it cool until it's semisolid. Pour your second layer and let cool; continue until your mold is filled. Try tilting them, too!

Diaries have little locks and keys with pink hearts on them, and your little brother finds them and reads them to his friends. Journals have gorgeous covers, no locks or frills, and look sophisticated enough to fool your brother and his friends into thinking there's no real juicy stuff inside (you know better, of course!). Unfortunately, those cool-looking blank books that they sell in bookstores are really expensive. But since you're on the D.I.Y. track, you can cover your own journals and personalize them to boot! Just no locks, please!

What You Need:

- **Medium-size school notebook, either spiral-bound or a composition notebook (black-and-white cover)**

- **Several sheets of decorated paper or origami paper**

- **Decoupage medium or white glue mixed with water**

- **Foam brush or paintbrush**

- **Scissors**

- **Pencil or flat wooden spatula**

- **Glue (optional)**

- **Glitter, fake flowers, small toys or other accoutrements for decorating (optional)**

How To Do It:

1 If you are covering a small spiral-bound notebook, butt the end of the paper against the wire spiral and cut a piece of paper large enough to overhang three edges of the cover by about 1", and repeat for the back cover. For a composition notebook, wrap the paper around the spine and onto the back cover. Chances are your paper will not wrap all the way around the book, so use another sheet for the back cover and overlap the seam by at least ½". On the back of the paper, mark where the corners of the cover are.

2 Put the front-cover paper facedown. Coat the front cover of the notebook with a generous amount of decoupage medium and center it on the paper, lining the corners up with your marks. Make sure the paper is aligned correctly. Roll the pencil along the cover or rub gently with the wooden spatula to help smooth out any air bubbles and extra goop.

3 Snip the corners of the overhang diagonally. Open the cover and brush a thin coat of decoupage medium on the overhanging bits. Fold in the two short ends of the paper first, making a nice crease at the edges. Glue down flaps, smoothing out any air bubbles. Let dry. Cut off any leftover triangles of paper. Repeat for the back cover.

4 If you're using a composition notebook, glue down the paper covering the spine the same way, cutting away any excess paper along the spine edges.

5 Cut two pieces of paper about ½" smaller than the inside front and back covers and use the decoupage medium to glue them on, making sure to butt the inside edge against the spiral binding or interior papers. Let dry.

6 Coat the front and back covers with a thin layer of decoupage medium. While the goop is wet, you can sprinkle glitter into it. Let dry.

7 Glue on fake flowers, small toys, or other pieces of paper in a cool design. Remember, the simpler the design, the more your nifty paper shows through.

For your vegan friends:

Use torn brown paper bags and overlap the edges to get a cool worn-leather look.

Cool-looking papers:

Look in the scrapbook section of the craft store for funky decorated papers or use pictures torn from magazines.

Dress It Up!

Feeling guilty about those clothes you haven't worn for seasons? Don't toss them! Give them a face-lift!

Hip Clips

HOW EASY? ✂

Sparkly things are good. And sparkly things in your hair are even better. Stop dropping all your hard-earned cash on boring barrettes and clips at the mall and make some sassy little doodads on your own.

What You Need:

- **Bobby pins or barrettes**

- **Clear-drying glue**

- **Beads of several different sizes**

- **Piece of cardboard**

How To Do It:

1 Slide the bobby pins or barrettes onto the piece of cardboard, flat side up.

2 Run a line of glue along the flat side of the bobby pin and press beads into the glue. Line up the holes of the beads so they're all facing in the same direction. Wipe away any excess glue. Let dry.

Funk it up:

- Coat the flat side of a small barrette with glue, and press beads into the glue.

- For a larger barrette, glue marble magnets (sans magnets) and beads onto the flat side.

Sparkly and Cheap!

Most bracelets and necklaces are pretty simple—beads strung on something. The hardest part about making your own jewelry is finding the beads. Luckily, bead, craft, fabric, and needlepoint stores abound, and you can even mine thrift shop jewelry for the beads and pendants. The cool thing about beading is that there are a ton of things to string beads onto, including elastic cord, nylon-coated wire (or Tiger Tail), and memory wire. Oh, and don't forget there are about a million designs you can make!

TO STRING AN ELASTIC NECKLACE

HOW EASY? ✂

What You Need:

• **Beads**

• **Clear beading elastic**

• **Needle with a small eye**

• **Clear nail polish**

• **Scissors**

• **Needle threader (optional)**

> **TIP** Use an egg carton to help hold and sort your beads while you're stringing.

How To Do It:

1 Cut a length of elastic at least 6" longer than you want the necklace or bracelet to be. Thread the needle with the elastic. This is the trickiest part.

2 Tie a knot in the elastic, about 2" from the end. Make sure it's bigger than the holes in your beads. Dab a little clear nail polish on the knot and let it dry.

3 String your beads in a pretty pattern until you reach the length you want your necklace to be.

4 Unthread the needle and tie the two ends of the thread together. Knot it securely, and dab clear nail polish on the knot to secure it. Run the excess thread back through the beads for an inch or two.

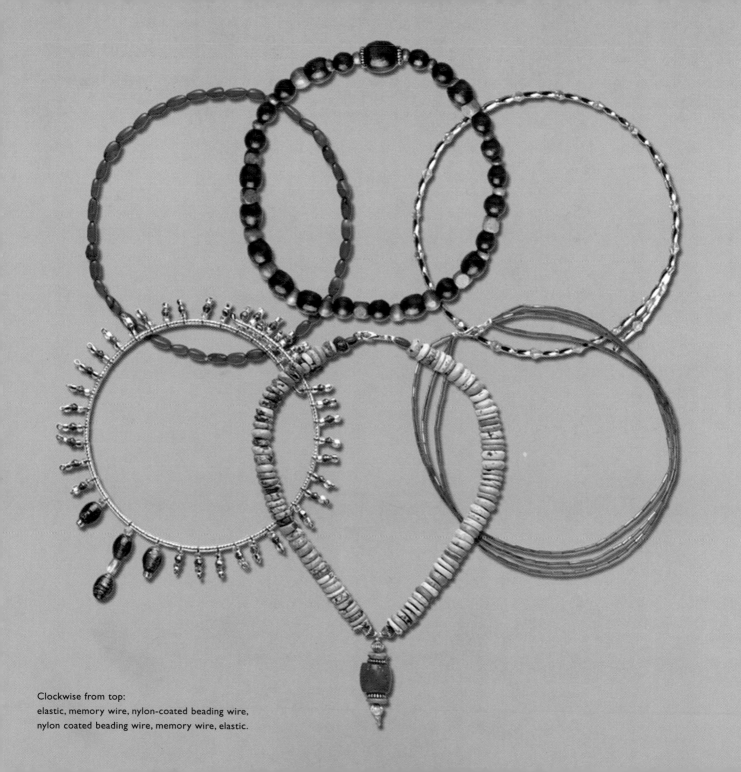

Clockwise from top:
elastic, memory wire, nylon-coated beading wire,
nylon coated beading wire, memory wire, elastic.

What You Need:

- **Beads**

- **Memory wire**

- **Pliers**

How To Do It:

1 Use the wire cutter on the pliers to cut a length of wire 1" longer than you want the necklace to be. Try it on first, as the wire sits differently than other necklaces.

2 Using the pliers, bend a small loop at the end of the memory wire. Make sure the end isn't poking out, or it'll scratch whoever wears the necklace.

3 Thread your beads on the wire.

4 Form another small loop at the end, and trim the wire end flush. You don't need a clasp since the wire has a memory and will spring back into place. (Memory wire, get it?)

42

What You Need:

- **Beads**

- **Nylon-coated wire, also known as Tiger Tail or Beadalon®**

- **2-piece clasp or a clasp and a jump ring (see supplies)**

- **2 crimp beads**

- **Pliers or tweezers**

- **Scissors**

How To Do It:

1. Cut a length of nylon-coated wire 4" longer than you want your necklace to be.

2. Thread one bead, one crimp bead, and half the clasp onto the wire. Bend about 1" of the wire around and go back through the crimp bead and bead and pull snug. Smoosh the crimp bead gently with the pliers or tweezers to hold it secure.

3. Thread a few more beads onto the wire and trim the short end. Thread the rest of your beads onto the wire.

4. Add one crimp bead and the other half of the clasp. Bend the wire down and back through the crimp bead and one or two other beads and gently pull snug, using the tweezers or pliers to help you. Smoosh the crimp bead gently with the pliers or tweezers and trim the end of the wire.

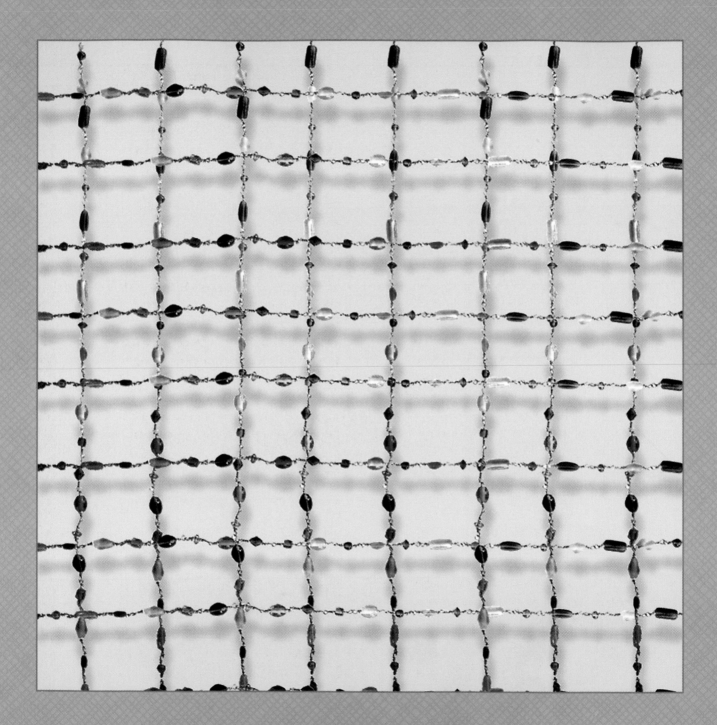

What You Need:

- **Beads**

- **Wire, thin enough to fit in the bead holes**

- **2-piece clasp**

- **Pliers**

How To Do It:

1 This necklace is done in sections. Cut an 18" piece of wire. Use the pliers to grab the wire about 1" from the free end and bend to a right angle. Slide half of the clasp onto the wire.

2 Grip the wire ¼" from the bend and turn the pliers to form a small loop, catching the clasp in the loop. Grab the loop with pliers and wrap the end around the wire below the loop a few times. Trim the extra wire.

3 String about ½" to ¾" worth of beads onto the wire. Push the beads flush to the wrapped end, and make another loop with the other end of the wire, wrapping the wire close to the beads. Snip the wire close to the wrap. You've got one unit done!

4 Thread the wire through the loop of the finished unit about 1", and bend the end at a right angle. Make a small loop, and wrap as decribed above to attach the wire to the unit.

5 Thread more beads onto the wire, push the beads flush to the wrapped end, and make another loop and wrap. Snip the wire flush.

6 Keep on making units and attaching them as you go. When the length of wire you're working with gets too short, start with another 18" piece.

7 When you get to the last unit, attach one end of the unit to the necklace and thread the beads and the other half of the clasp onto the wire. Catch the clasp in the end loop, wrap, and trim.

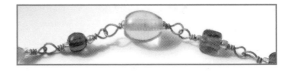

TIP When working with wire, work in 18" lengths to make the sections. It's easier to work with a longer length, and you'll waste less wire.

Fancy Footwork

FAKE FLOWER FLIP-FLOPS

HOW EASY? ✂

OK, these are so easy, and they sell for so much, it ought to be criminal. They literally take less than five minutes to make, so they're the perfect dress-me-up project for when you're running out the door to the beach. Seriously, they're so easy, I almost feel bad for those fancy-pants shoe people, because everyone and their mother can make these suckers.

What You Need:

- **A pair of flip-flops**

- **Fake flowers**

- **Scissors**

- **Clear-drying glue or glue gun**

- **Lace or ribbon trim (optional)**

How To Do It:

1 Pull the fake flowers off the stems and use the scissors to trim off that little plastic dweedlebobber on the base of the flowers.

2 Wrap and glue ribbon around the straps, or glue on lace trim before you attach the flower.

3 Make sure the flip-flops are clean, and glue the flowers onto the straps. Glue as many or as few as you want.

Update Your Look

HOW EASY? ✂ ✂

Your mom's been bugging you to clean out your closet for weeks now, but you can't bear to part with those super comfy, but super ratty jeans. Or your camis are all sooo last year, and new ones cost major bucks. Whatever is a girl to do? Well, run to the fabric store and get your hands on some trims—you know, rick-rack, woven ribbon, fringe, lace, whatever you can find that looks pretty. One or two yards will only run you a couple of bucks, and combined with a little fabric glue and some creativity, you can have a whole new wardrobe in an afternoon!

What You Need:

- Approximately 1 yard of fabric trim (or enough to go once around whatever it is you're decking out)

- Washable fabric glue, like Aleene's® OK to Wash It®

- Scissors

- Piece of plain paper

- Masking tape

How To Do It:

1 First, decide what you're going to decorate. See the sidebar for some ideas. Use a couple of different trims or lace in similar colors, or just run one line of trim around the hem, top edge, or waistband.

2 Lay out your design first, without cutting the trim. If you're running short on trims, just work on the front. If you're using fringe, look and see if you want the top edge of the fringe to show or if you want to glue it to the inside of the garment and let the fringe hang.

3 Once you have your layout, fold the end of the trim under itself about $1/4$" and use the glue to secure. Slip the piece of paper inside the garment so you don't accidentally glue the front to the back.

4 Start at a side seam, or other inconspicuous place. Working in 4" to 5" sections at a time, run a line of glue on the back side of the trim and press firmly in place. Wipe up any glue that seeps out.

5 Rip off a piece of masking tape and tape in place. Work your way around the piece, wiping and taping as you go. The glue generally sets in three to five minutes, after which you can take the tape off. Let dry for 24 hours.

Inspiration Central

- **Run trim down the sides of the sleeves of a long-sleeve T-shirt.**

- **Forget the fringe at the hems of your capris, and glue three layers of fringe around the top of your cami. Just make sure to butt the top edge of the second layer right against the bottom edge of the first.**

- **Glue several different lace trims vertically to the front of a white camisole for a cool vintage look. Glue more lace to the straps.**

TIP Make sure to wash the item inside out on gentle, and air dry so you don't ruin your decorations.

Go crazy and be creative. Sometimes the weirdest combinations look the coolest. Try **EVERYTHING**. Just lay it out first to see if you like it before you cut and glue.

Dream Skirt

PILLOWCASE SKIRT

Pillowcases make perfect skirts. Not only are they already hemmed and stitched up the sides so all you need to do is make a waistband, but they come in random funky colors. Grab a lace-edged pillowcase for a sweet little summer skirt, or steal that old Incredible Hulk pillowcase from your brother and make a funky original. Just remember that since you're turning the case on end, whatever pattern you pick will be turned on its side, too.

What You Need:

- **1 pillowcase**

- **¼ yard fusible (iron-on) interfacing**

- **Needle and thread or sewing machine**

- **2 yards narrow ribbon, rickrack, or seam binding**

- **Scissors**

- **Ruler**

- **Safety pin**

- **Iron**

How To Do It:

1 Iron the pillowcase flat, cut 2" off the closed end, and turn inside out.

2 Cut a piece of fusible or iron-on interfacing 2" wide and long enough to go all the way around the cut edge of the pillowcase tube.

3 Bumpy (glue) side down, iron the interfacing onto the inside cut edge of the tube, aligning the edges. Press for at least 10 seconds in each area to get a good bond.

4 Fold down 1" of the interfaced edge and press flat. Sew in place along the lower edge, leaving at least ¼" seam allowance. Turn right (a.k.a. pretty) side out. This is a casing or channel for your drawstring.

5 Decide which side of the pillowcase you want to be the front and measure to find the exact center front. Snip a small slit in the top layer of the casing, being careful not to cut the stitching or into the back layer.

6 Cut a piece of ribbon long enough to go around the pillowcase plus a foot for your drawstring. Pin the safety pin to one end of the ribbon and thread it all the way through the casing.

7 Take off the safety pin and try on the skirt. Trim the ends of the ribbon to the length you want it and tie knots at the ends so they don't get lost in the casing.

TIP Can't fit into a pillowcase? Well, thanks to genetics and some nice childbearing hips, neither can I. But I still have a Star Wars skirt because I grabbed a second pillowcase (or ½ yard of a coordinating fabric) and added pieces in. Cut one rectangle 2" longer than the case and wide enough to make it fit over your butt. Fold one end up 1", and press. Fold up another inch, press and sew down to make a hem. After cutting the end off the tube, but before the interfacing, slit one side seam of the case. Holding right sides together and matching hemmed edges, sew the rectangle into the open case on both sides to form a wider tube. Follow the rest of the directions at left, centering the inserted rectangle in the center front or center back of the skirt when you cut the hole for the casing.

The Softer Side of Denim

DENIM SKIRT

HOW EASY? ✂ ✂

We have here a simple pair of jeans. Maybe a little done, but once a favorite. Say the magic words. . . . Oooh, now they're a skirt! It's magic, magic, I tell you! OK, maybe not magic, but it is a pretty quick and easy project.

What You Need:

- **An old pair of jeans that still fit in the waist and hips**

- **½ yard of cool fabric**

- **Sewing machine or needle and thread**

- **Straight pins**

- **Scissors**

- **Brown paper bag, or other large sheet of paper**

- **Pencil**

> **TIP** You can sew this skirt by hand. But to make your life that much easier, ask to borrow your mom's sewing machine. Mom doesn't sew? Check out a friend, a friend's mom, cousin, uncle, grandma, neighbor, random strangers on the street. OK, not that last one.

How To Do It:

1 Button up the jeans and lay them flat on the floor. Notice how the legs form a triangle? That's where the fabric will go. Cut the legs open at the inside seam (inseam). Cut on one side of the thick flat-fell seam so that it falls to the front of the skirt.

2 The jeans won't lie flat until you cut a few inches up the crotch seam on both the front and back. Flip the jeans over and snip along one side of the back crotch seam a little at a time. Lap one piece over the other and keep snipping until the back lies fairly flat. You will have to cut pretty far up the seam to get rid of the bubble. Once it lies flat, use the straight pin, duct or masking tape to hold the overlapping pieces in place.

3 Flip the jeans back over and snip and overlap the front crotch seam the same way. You won't have to go as far to make the front lie flat, and be careful not to cut too far and hit the fly. Pin in place.

4 Sew the front and back overlaps in place, about ¼" from the edges. For security, sew a second line of stitching about ¼" from the first line. When the edges fray—and they will—the two lines will keep the skirt from falling apart. Turn the jeans inside out and trim the loose hanging overlaps to 1" from the stitching.

5 Turn the jeans right side out. Cut open a brown paper bag and lay it inside the jeans. Trace the opening onto the paper, then add 2" all around. Cut out your tracing, pin it to the fabric, and cut around it. Cut around the tracing again for the second triangle.

6 Slip one triangle faceup into the jeans and center it so the excess fabric is even and hidden inside. Pin the jeans and fabric together near the edge. (Easiest way: stick the straight pins standing up into the sandwich of fabric, then with one hand inside the jeans to guide the pins, poke them back up and through the jeans and fabric.) Sew with two lines of stitching ¼" apart, ¼" from the edge of the denim. Do the same for the back with the second triangle.

7 Try on your skirt—it will be WAY too long. Use a mirror or a friend to help mark where you want it, and cut off the excess length, leaving an extra inch if you want a hemmed skirt.

8 To hem, turn the extra inch up into the skirt and sew down. If you want a frayed hem, sew two lines of stitching about ¼" apart and 1" from the bottom of the skirt.

Be a Rock Star (or just look like one)

HOW EASY? ✂ ✂ ✂

Nowadays, you can get anything for your computer. But the coolest thing is T-shirt transfer paper. This is the same paper that makes the nifty little retro designs on those T-shirts that every indie rocker is wearing. Take your favorite saying, that inside joke with your friends, or even your name, and make it into a one-of-a-kind original, and let everyone think that you're a rock star.

What You Need:

- **T-shirt**

- **Computer**

- **Color printer**

- **Sheet of T-shirt transfer paper for color printers**

- **Iron**

- **Scissors**

- **Glitter fabric paint and mini-rhinestones (optional)**

- **Fabric jewel/stud glue (optional)**

How To Do It:

1 Decide what your design will be. Words are easiest to start out with, but you can also take pictures off the Internet or scan in photos and whatnot.

2 If you are using words, you'll need to reverse or mirror them on the computer or at your local copy shop. Print the design onto plain paper first to see how it lays on the shirt and how the color(s) print out.

3 Follow the directions on the package of transfer paper to see which side you need to print on. In most cases, you will have to make sure the image prints on the dull side of the paper. Print out your image.

4 Cut out around your design. If you like, you can cut out the blank, unprinted areas inside your design. If you've used words, you can cut out the entire phrase or around each letter individually. Be aware that any unprinted areas will transfer as clear to the shirt and be slightly shiny.

5 Put the T-shirt on a hard, flat surface (protect a floor or table with a thin towel). Iron the fabric without steam, to remove any wrinkles or creases and to preheat the fabric.

6 Lay your design, printed side down, on the fabric, and press the iron (no steam) firmly over the transfer for as long as recommended on the package, usually 15 to 20 seconds.

7 Follow the package directions as to when to peel the backing off. In general, peeling the paper off while the fabric is still hot gives a slightly matte or satin finish and peeling when cool gives a very shiny or glossy finish.

8 Add accents or outline with the glitter fabric paint and glue on rhinestones for sparkle. I made the shirt above for my friend Sharren by transferring her name, outlining each letter and an oval with paint, and making a little ™ symbol with rhinestones. Now she's a logo! (But not officially.)

> **TIP** Regular T-shirt transfer paper works best on white or light-colored T-shirts. If you're jonesing to transform that basic black tee, keep an eye out for opaque transfer paper, which will really make the colors pop.

Don't have a computer?

Or a color printer or scanner? Don't sweat it! Take your design to a copy shop (most are open 24 hours for those late-night crafty fits) and print it out there, or have them color copy it onto transfer paper. Many shops actually have transfer paper available. Just get your design perfect at home, or else you'll be paying for that tinkering time on the computer.

Tough Tees

PUNK T-SHIRT

"Deconstructed" clothes are super trendy. Even the fashion houses are taking thrift store finds, ripping them, and gussying them up with doodads. Of course their stuff is selling for literally thousands of dollars, but you can do the exact same thing at home with some scissors and a little imagination.

What You Need:

- An old T-shirt, preferably one with a design on it

- Scissors

- Seam binding or 1"-wide ribbon

- Shoelace or narrow ribbon

- Needle and thread to match the shirt

- Flat-backed jewels

- Jewel fabric glue

- Pronged studs

- Thimble

- Colored chalk

How To Do It:

1 Lay the tee flat and cut off the collar at the seam. Try the shirt on and mark with the colored chalk where you want the neckline to go.

2 Take the shirt off and cut just inside the chalk line. T-shirt fabric rolls and won't fray, so you don't need to hem it.

3 Cut off the hems of the sleeves, and snip up the outside of the sleeves to the shoulder seam, making sure not to cut into the shoulders. Snip a slight angle along the cut edge to soften the right angles of the new flutter sleeve.

4 Cut off the hem of the T-shirt body and turn the shirt inside out. Cut four pieces of seam binding or 1"-wide ribbon to fit under the sleeves to the hem. Two pieces will be sewn on either side of the shirt's side seam to make a casing for the narrower ribbon or shoelace. Using a running stitch, sew up one long edge of seam binding, right next to the side seam of the shirt. Lay a

long piece of narrow ribbon underneath the casing and sew across the top of the casing and ribbon, securing the ribbon at the top. Sew down the other edge of the casing, being careful not to catch the narrow ribbon. Trim the casing about ¼" below the bottom of the shirt, and leave the narrow ribbon long. Do the same on the other side of the side seam. Repeat for the other side of the shirt, making four casings with ribbon attached. Trim the narrow ribbon to within 4" inches of the hem.

5   To scrunch the sides of the shirt, hold the narrow ribbons and gather each side up as much as you want. Tie the two ribbons on each side to hold the gathers up.

6   Follow the design of the T-shirt, or make your own, and glue on the flat-backed jewels with the jewel fabric glue. Make sure to embed all edges of the jewel in the glue. Let dry.

7   Add the pronged studs, poking them through the fabric of the shirt and using the thimble to bend the prongs inward, securing the stud.

> **TIP**   Wash inside out on delicate and air dry so you don't destroy your work of art!

OK, this was a really busy shirt.

Not a fan of the shiny things? Skip the jewels, studs, and glitter. Can't sew worth a darn? This kind of sewing isn't hard, but you can just leave the sides of the shirt alone and go nuts decorating the front. Any way you cut it, you still have a cool deconstructed tee.

For All You Bag Ladies...

BASIC RECTANGLE BAG

I love purses. I have about a million of them, most of them handmade. They're quick, require a minimum amount of sewing, and if you use old wool sweaters you've felted down in the washing machine, super cheap. Felting keeps the ends from fraying and looks all warm and cozy to boot. If you're not a wool-sweater-wearing kind of gal, raid your dad's closet (ask first!), look for old 100% wool sweaters at thrift stores and garage sales, or just skip the sweater thing and grab about ¾ yard of cool fabric.

What You Need:

- **An old 100% wool sweater**

- **Needle**

- **Embroidery floss**

- **Scissors**

- **Ruler**

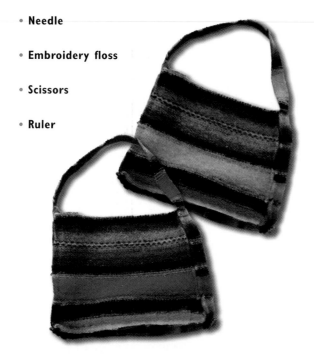

How To Do It:

1 Start by felting the wool sweater. It must be 100% wool, angora, alpaca, mohair, cashmere, or a mix of these in order to felt. Sweaters labeled machine wash and dry, acrylic, cotton, linen, or rayon just will not work. Wash the sweater on the hottest wash cycle possible with a couple of towels or pairs of jeans, then dry on the hottest setting possible. Do this until the sweater is thick, dense, and you can no longer make out the individual stitches.

2 Cut out two 8½" x 11" rectangles from the sweater for the body of the bag. Cut two 8½" x 3" rectangles for the sides of the bag, and one 3" x 11" rectangle for the bottom of the bag. Cut a 22" x 1" rectangle from the sleeves of the sweater for the strap. If your sweater isn't long enough for the strap, cut two 11" x 1" rectangles.

3 This bag has seams that show, so hold wrong (a.k.a. ugly) sides together, sew the short side of one side piece to the short side of the bottom, ½" from the edge. Sew the short side of the other side piece to the other side of the bottom, making sure the seam is facing the same way (sticky-outy part out).

4 Matching 8½" sides and holding wrong sides together, sew one body piece to one side, then the bottom, then the other side. The bottom corner will be a toughie, so use the needle to poke the corner of the body piece into place. Do the same with the other body piece.

5 You now have the body of the bag finished! The strap is up next. If you cut the strap in two sections, hold the two pieces right (a.k.a. pretty) sides together, and sew ½" from the edges. Do two layers of stitching, one on top of the other if it doesn't feel secure. Alternately, you can butt the edges and whipstitch them together, or lap one end over the other by about 1" and sew two rows of stitching ¼" apart.

6 Sew one end of the strap to the side piece of the bag on the inside, overlapping the pieces about 1" and sewing ¼" from the edges. Sew across the top of the bag, down the side, across the bottom and up the other side, to make a box for the most secure strap. Do the same for the other side, making sure the strap isn't twisted.

Some fun variations:

Instead of sewing with a running stitch, whipstitch the edges of the seams. You don't have to have the seams on the outside, just hold right (a.k.a. pretty) sides together when you sew; turn your bag inside out and press the seams crisp with a hot steam iron. Change around the strap. Cut different lengths, use an old belt, or pick up a length of chain from the hardware store. Add a flap. Cut one side of the body of the bag 14" x 11½" and let the extra 5½" flap over the opening.

TIP **Don't cut your embroidery floss longer than about 20", otherwise it will tangle.**

Jeans. Is There Anything They Can't Do?

HOW EASY? ✂ ✂

So now that you've mastered the basic bag pattern, move on up to recycling your old jeans into a super-cool messenger bag. Hey, built-in pockets!

What You Need:

- **An old pair of jeans**

- **Needle and embroidery floss or sewing machine**

- **Scissors**

- **Iron**

- **Ribbon (optional)**

How To Do It:

1 Zip up and button the jeans and lay them on the floor. Cut the legs straight across just below the crotch. Save the legs!

2 Decide whether you want the bottom seam to be hidden, or out in the open and fraying. If you want a hidden seam, turn the jeans inside out and, holding right sides together, sew the legs shut ½" from the edge. To make sure the seam is stable, sew a second line ¼" from the edge. If you want a fraying seam, make sure the jeans are right side out. Holding wrong (ugly) sides together, sew the bottom shut 1" from the edge, then sew second line right next to the first. Iron the seam flat.

3 Slit one leftover leg open at the inside seam, or inseam. Decide whether you want that thick flat-fell seam on your strap, if you want the strap to fray or not, and how long you want it to be. If you're using the seam on the strap, be sure to center it so you won't have to sew through it (that's a really thick piece of denim).

4   If you want a fraying strap, cut two rectangles 2¾" wide by whatever length you want the strap to be plus 4". Holding wrong sides together and matching ends, sew the strap together on the two long sides. Run two lines of stitching right next to each other, and ½" from the edge. Iron flat.

5   If you want a nonfraying strap, cut one rectangle 5½" wide by whatever length you want it to be plus 4". Fold in half, right sides together, and sew along the long side, ½" from the edge. Run two lines of stitching ¼" apart for stability. Turn right side out and iron flat.

6   Lay the body of your bag down flat, center the button and fly, and sew the strap to the interior sides of the bag, overlapping 2". Sew across the top edge, down the side of the overlap, across the bottom and up the other side, ¼" from the edge. Run a second line of stitching next to the first. Repeat for the other side.

7   Tack the jeans shut at the button so random strangers can't unbutton your bag. Leave the fly zipper functional for easy access.

8   If you want a closure, cut a strip of ribbon about 6" long. Overlap the ends and sew to the jeans label on the inside of the bag, making a loop that will slide over the jeans button.

TIP   You don't have to use a sewing machine for this project, but just be aware that denim is pretty thick and very tough.

Decor Diva

Sick of kickin' it in the same old digs? Liven up your lounge space!

Picture This

HOW EASY? ✂

Forget albums, show off your photos in frames worthy of their gorgeousness! Pick up some cheap wood or plastic frames at a dollar or discount store, or recycle your own frames and outdo Pottery Barn.

What You Need:

- **Cheap picture frames**

- **Acrylic paint**

- **Foam brush**

- **Clear-drying glue**

- **Decoupage medium**

- **Flat glass marbles, or beads, or images from magazines or decorated paper, or a brown paper bag**

1 Take the glass and mat out of the frame.

2 Paint the frame in a background color. I usually go for silver or black, but go crazy and pick that wild neon color if you want.

3 To make a marble frame: Glue flat-backed marbles around the frame with clear-drying glue. Try using marbles with images glued to the back (see page 7).

4 To make a beaded frame: Coat a 2" to 3" section of the frame with a thick layer of clear-drying glue and lay your beads into it in a pretty design. Let it set for a minute. Work around the frame, letting each section set a bit before moving onto the next. Or pour tiny beads out on a sheet of paper, and set a glue-coated picture frame in the beads. Press the beads firmly into the glue.

5 To make a decoupaged frame: Brush a layer of decoupage medium on the frame in small sections and press images or decorated paper into the goop. Smooth out air bubbles and form the image to the frame with your fingers. Brush another layer of medium on top to seal the edges.

6 To make the brown paper bag frame: Tear up the bag into 2" to 3" pieces, dampen with a little water, and crumple them up. Working in sections, glue the pieces to the frame with decoupage medium, overlapping the torn edges. Brush more decoupage

medium on top and let dry. The edges of the bag meld together and all the crinkles make the paper look like distressed leather.

Personalize Your Boudoir

LAMP SHADES

Nothing is more boring than a plain old white lamp shade, and no one wants to drop a ton of cash on those fancy ones. Why not decorate your own with some paint and glue and dress up your dressing room? It's easy and won't take very long, either.

What You Need:

- **An old lamp shade**

- **Acrylic paint in your favorite color(s)**

- **Metallic acrylic paint (optional)**

- **Clear-drying glue**

- **Ribbon or trim**

- **Scissors**

- **Foam brush or paintbrush**

- **Masking tape**

How To Do It:

1 Clean the lamp shade so that it's free of any dust and dirt. If you want, paint the inside of the lamp shade with the metallic paint. Silver adds a nice reflective glow, and gold gives a warmer light. Let dry.

2 Paint the entire outside of the shade and let dry.

3 In a contrasting shade of paint, add squiggles, dots, or other designs. Use the masking tape to mask off straight lines and shapes. Let dry.

4 Cut the ribbon or trim to go around the top edge of the shade, leaving 1" extra. Fold the raw edge under ½" and glue around the top of the shade, butting the edges together. Do the same for the bottom edge, making sure the seams are on the same side. Let dry.

5 If you have fringe or hanging trim, glue that to the inside bottom edge of the shade.

ROUND AND ROUND

Paint the shade a base color and glue several sizes of ribbon around the outside, leaving anywhere between ½" and 2" of background color in between.

KNOW YOUR ABCS

Paint the shade a base color. Print or photo copy large letters, and decoupage them onto the shade at random. Seal with a clear acrylic sealer.

MOCK STAINED GLASS

Rip up various colors of tissue paper and decoupage onto the shade, overlapping the edges slightly. Use a black permanent marker to outline geometric or stained glass designs. Seal with acrylic sealer. When the light shines through, it looks like stained glass.

THE LEATHER LOOK

Rip up a brown paper bag to decoupage onto the shade, overlapping the edges. Seal with a matte acrylic sealer.

PICTURE PERFECT

Decoupage magazine images (fave celebs or fun ads) or decorative paper onto the shade and seal with acrylic sealer.

Light Up Your Life

BOTTLE LAMP

HOW EASY? ✂

Everyone loves Christmas lights, so keep 'em on display all year long.

What You Need:

- **A clear or translucent glass vase, at least 10" high**

- **String of Christmas lights**

- **Lamp shade**

- **Extension cord or power strip (optional)**

How To Do It:

1 Clean the vase inside and out. Decorate, if you like, with frosty paint "etching" (see page 16).

2 Put the string of lights into the vase, letting the plug end trail out.

3 Set the lamp shade on top of the vase, and plug in. If necessary, use an extension cord or power strip so you can set the lamp where you like.

TIP Look in hardware stores for a plug-in switch. Plug the lights into the switch, and the switch into the wall, so you can flick your lamp on and off.

Clip-on lamp shades work best for this kind of lamp as the clip part can rest on top of the vase and keep the shade from sinking down too far.

71

Hang It Up

BULLETIN BOARD

Don't want to ruin that prom picture by sticking a pushpin in it? Grab some foam core and fabric and whip up this sassy little bulletin board that won't destroy any of your photos or concert stubs—and it'll look totally classy and expensive. Just slip the photo or keepsake under the ribbons and enjoy!

What You Need:

- **1 sheet of foam core, approximately 20" x 30"**

- **Batting 3" larger than the foam core**

- **1 yard of fabric**

- **3 yards of 1"-wide ribbon**

- **Thumbtacks**

- **1 picture hanger**

- **Glue or glue gun**

- **Scissors**

- **Ruler**

- **Pencil or chalk**

> **TIP** When gluing the batting and fabric down, use tape or the pushpins to hold one side in place while you pull the other side taut.
>
> If the fabric or batting wants to unfold while the glue is drying, tape or pin in place until dry.

1 Place the foam core on the batting, centering it so the overhang is even all around. Starting in the center of one side and pulling the batting taut and even, glue the batting to the back of the foam core. Pull the batting from the opposite side as you glue, to get rid of wrinkles. Fold the corners neatly, and let dry. Trim off excess batting.

2 Cut a piece of fabric 4" larger than the foam core and lay it facedown. Center the batting-covered foam core, batting side down, on top. Glue down as above for the batting, making sure there are no wrinkles and the corners look neat. Let dry and trim off the excess fabric.

3 Place the board fabric side up, and measure the diagonals. Mark 5 equal spaces along both diagonals (see photo), and draw the 10 lines on the fabric and down the edges. The ribbon will cover the lines, but use a light touch.

4 Cut a length of ribbon long enough to run across the front of the board on the diagonal and extend about 2" onto the back of the board. Secure one end of the ribbon with glue on the back of the board at one mark, and run it up, over, and down across the board following the line. Pull the ribbon taut but not super tight, and secure on the back with glue. Do the same for each marked line, securing the ribbon ends on the back of the board with glue. Let dry.

5 Add a dab of glue to the underside of the thumbtack and press into the board at the center of each ribbon intersection. Let dry.

6 Attach the picture hanger to the back of the board with strong glue or glued thumbtacks.

Forget Me...NOT!

Can't remember to tie your shoes? Always forgetting your homework, or worse, your cell phone? Put some empty space to work and string this nifty, next-to-invisible reminder holder across a doorway, window, or closet. Since you're putting holes into woodwork, just make sure you ask permission from the nearest mortgage-paying or rent-paying member of the household. Oh, and hang it high enough so you don't clothesline someone with your notes.

What You Need:

- **3'–4' of fishing line, or a length 6" longer than your chosen opening**

- **2 ½" eyehooks, available at a hardware store**

- **10–15 small bulldog or binder clips**

- **Nail**

- **Ruler**

- **Pencil**

How To Do It:

1 Measure down about 3" from the top of the opening your bulletin board will span and mark on each side where your eyehooks will go.

2 Use the nail to make an indent on each mark, then screw in both eyehooks.

TIP You can also string the binder clips onto the fishing line through the metal "handles" before tying the line up.

3 Tie one end of the fishing line to one eyehook, and stretch the line taut across the opening. Tie the free end to the other eyehook.

4 Clip the binder clips over the fishing line and watch your notes float in midair!

75

Slumber in Style

Pillow covers do a lot to jazz up your bedroom, and they're easy to make by slapping two squares together. But sometimes a plain old pillow cover just isn't enough. Flash back to grade-school weaving with some cool satiny ribbons, and make a pillow cover worthy of a princess.

What You Need:

- **An old 16" x 16" pillow or pillow form**

- **5 yards each of 6 different ribbons of various colors and widths**

- **1 yard of fusible interfacing**

- **Straight pins**

- **Masking tape**

- **Needle and thread or sewing machine**

- **Iron**

- **Brown paper bag**

- **Pencil**

- **Ruler**

- **Scissors**

How To Do It:

1 Open the paper bag flat and use the ruler to draw a 33" x 17" rectangle. Cut it out on the lines. This will be the pattern for the pillow cover. It matches the dimensions of the pillow plus $\frac{1}{2}$" seam allowance all around.

2 Decide in what order you want your ribbons. Cut enough 34" lengths of ribbon to span 18" when laid side by side. Cut enough 18" lengths to span 34".

3 Working on a towel, lay out the 34"-long ribbons facedown in your selected pattern. Make sure there are no spaces between the ribbons and that the top edge is fairly even. Tape down the top edge so it's secure.

4 Start weaving the 18" lengths, making sure the ribbons are facedown. Use straight pins or pieces of masking tape to secure the ends. Remember, over, under, over, under…

5 When you've woven all your lengths, double-check the piece to make sure there are no gaps between the ribbons and that they are all lying smooth and flat. Cut a piece of fusible interfacing as large as your ribbon fabric and lay it bumpy (glue) side down. Use the iron to fuse the interfacing to the ribbons, starting from the center of the ribbons to the edges. Press for at least 10 seconds in each spot to get a good bond.

6 When cool, pull up the tape and flip over your new fabric. Pin your brown paper bag pattern to the fabric, and cut out around it.

7 Fold the fabric in half, ribbon sides together. Align the cut edges, press flat.

8 Sew around two sides of the pillow $\frac{1}{2}$" from the edge. Turn right side out and press flat.

9 Insert the pillow, fold the open edges in $\frac{1}{2}$", pin, and sew the opening shut by hand.

> **TIP** Start with a small pillow, or you'll be weaving forever.
>
> Feeling adventurous? Use another size pillow form, adjusting your pattern to fit the dimensions of the pillow, or try a circular pillow.

Mosaic Madness

HOW EASY? ✂ ✂ ✂

I'll admit it. I'm a klutz. Dishes get broken whenever I am around. But here's a cool little table that can put those sad, sad shards to some kind of decorative use. And it's next to impossible for a klutz like me to screw up!

What You Need:

- **Several old dishes with pretty patterns—a sure thing at thrift stores and garage sales**

- **1 teacup or small bowl**

- **Strong glue, like liquid nails**

- **White or colored sanded grout**

- **Acrylic paint**

- **Foam brush or paintbrush**

- **Several paper bags**

- **Newspapers**

- **Hammer, rubber mallet, or other heavy object**

- **Sponge**

- **Rubber gloves**

1 Double or triple bag the paper bags. Place a few dishes at a time in the bag, and roll up the opening.
Working outside or in the garage, and wearing safety
glasses, lay the bag on several layers of newspaper and
put several more layers of newspaper on top. Use the
hammer or heavy object (clogs work particularly
well) to break the dishes into pieces. Whack lightly at
first until you get a feel how the plates break. You want
pieces about 1" to 3" each.

2 Take the pieces out of the bag and sort into usable
versus unusable pieces on some newspaper. Try not
to use any pieces with the heavy rim of the plate.
Keep at it until all your dishes, save the cup or bowl,
are broken. Hold onto the unusable pieces until
you're completely done with the mosaic, just in
case.

3 Clean the top of your table, and start laying out
your design. Place the cup or bowl first, and work
around it with the smaller pieces. Leave some space
between pieces, but try not to leave any gaps larger
than ¼" (here's where the unusable pieces may be
handy).

4 When you've got the design the way you like, glue
the cup or bowl down first, and work out from
there, gluing the pieces down. Don't be stingy with
the glue, but don't let excess glue overflow the tiles.
Let dry completely.

5 Once the top is completely dry, grab the grout. It comes in either dry mix or a premixed container. If you have a dry grout mix, follow the package directions and mix it with water in a disposable container.

6 Cover your work area with newspapers as this is a messy job. Using the sponge and wearing rubber gloves, cram the grout into all those little spaces, wiping or smooshing diagonally across the top. Try to avoid letting globs of grout sit on the top of the mosaic or on the rest of the table. Work pretty quickly, as you don't want the grout to set all the way up.

7 When you've got all the cracks filled, remove gloves and wet the sponge. Wring out most of the water and wipe down the top of the mosaic. Wipe on the diagonal whenever possible, and be careful not to dig the grout out of the cracks. Keep wiping and wringing out the sponge until the top is clean. Let dry.

8 Once the mosaic is dry, there's still probably going to be a haze. Just wipe that off with a damp sponge.

9 Paint the bottom half of the table. Don't worry if you get paint on the mosaic top—just wipe it up while it's still wet.

TIP Don't use substantially thicker pieces, or your top will be uneven. Minor thickness differences can be evened out using a heavy hand with the glue.

Rock-a-Bye Baby

HOW EASY? ✂ ✂ ✂

Got a ton of T-shirts you hardly ever wear, but can't bear to part with? Well, gather up those random tees and make a cozy quilt. Use your old concert tees with dates on the back, or take to the thrift stores and garage sales for some random vintage tees and make a funky quilt in one afternoon.

What You Need:

- **20 T-shirts**

- **1 full-size quilt batt**

- **Scissors**

- **Needle and thread to match shirts, or sewing machine**

- **10 yards 2"- or 3"-wide ribbon, or seam binding to match**

- **Embroidery floss or ¼" ribbon**

- **Straight or safety pins**

- **Ruler**

- **Iron**

How To Do It:

1 Iron all of the T-shirts to get rid of any wrinkles. For each shirt, slit up the side seams and cut off the sleeves. Cut the front and back apart at the shoulder seams. Measure out a 19" square on both the front and back, centering any image or pattern in the square. Cut out the front and back squares for each shirt. You should have 40 squares, 20 fronts and 20 backs.

2 Pick out 20 squares for the front of the quilt. You can pick all fronts, all backs, or a mix of fronts and backs. Lay out the squares on the floor, four across and five down.

3 Start at the top row, and working from left to right, pin the first square to the second square, right (a.k.a. pretty) sides together. Go across the entire row, pinning each square to the square next to it. Fold the pinned row up. Do this for each row, and put your five stacks aside.

4 Lay out, pin, and stack the remaining 20 squares for the back of the quilt. Set aside.

5 Starting with the first-row stack, and holding right sides together, sew the squares to each other along the pinned lines, $\frac{1}{2}$" from the edge. Make sure the edges are lined up. Iron each seam flat and open, so the seam allowances are folded back onto the wrong side of the block. Repeat for each pinned stack for both the front and the back of the quilt.

6 You now have five long strips for the front and five for the back. Lay out the front strips in order, and pin the first strip to the second, right sides together. Sew together, $\frac{1}{2}$" from the edge. Iron the seam flat and open.

7 Pin and sew the second strip to the third, and so forth, until the entire front of the quilt is pinned and sewn together. Repeat for the back of the quilt.

8 Now you have a big quilt top and a big quilt back, ready for the fluffy stuff. Lay the quilt back on the floor, facedown. Spread the quilt batt onto the back, and trim to the size of the back.

9 Lay the quilt front faceup on top of the batting, aligning edges with the quilt back. Pin the quilt sandwich together in a few places, and trim the excess batting.

10 Fold the ribbon in half, wrong sides in, and press flat. Fold under the ends of the ribbon $\frac{1}{2}$" and press flat. Start in the middle of one side and slip the quilt sandwich into the folded ribbon, so the raw edges are completely encased. Pin together, folding the corners neatly, and overlapping the ends of the ribbon where they meet. Sew in place through all the layers close to the inside edge of the ribbon.

11 Using the embroidery floss or $\frac{1}{4}$" ribbon, tack all the layers of the quilt together at the center of each block and at each intersection. Don't tie a knot at the end of the floss, and leave a 3" tail on the back of the quilt. Take two or three stitches right on top of each other, and tie a firm knot with the ends of the floss on the back of the quilt. Trim the ends.

Size matters:

Want to change the size of the quilt? Use a larger or smaller number of blocks per row.

Not Your Average Chalkboard

CHALKBOARD TABLE

HOW EASY? ✂ ✂

OK, Picasso. You stopped drawing on furniture when you retired your crayons, right? Well, take a gander at this cool little table with a chalkboard top perfect for your next masterpiece. This time, Mom won't get mad when you decide to "redecorate" your bedside table!

What You Need:

• **1 can chalkboard spray paint, or 1 quart brush-on chalkboard paint**

• **1 or more colors of acrylic paint**

• **An old table with a flat top**

• **Low-tack masking tape**

• **Newspapers**

• **Sanding paper**

• **Foam brush or paintbrush**

• **Chalk**

How To Do It:

1 Lightly sand your old table until the finish is dull and the surfaces are smooth. Clean off the dust.

2 Paint the bottom half and legs of the table with the acrylic paint. You may need more than one coat if you're using a light color. Be sure to let the paint dry completely between coats.

3 Take the table outside or into a well-ventilated area. Protect the floor and anything else nearby with newspapers—go out several feet around you just in case.

4 Tape newspapers around the painted half of the table to protect your paint. Spray or brush on at least two coats of the chalkboard paint. If you're using spray paint, make sure to hold the can at least 12" above the table and use several light coats rather than one heavy coat. Let dry completely between coats.

5 When completely dry, remove newspapers and start drawing!

TIP To keep from ripping off your paint with masking tape, use low-tack or painter's tape or tape newspapers to the underside of the tabletop. Remember, you can always touch up the table if you need to.

General craft, fabric, and art stores:

Joanne Fabrics and Crafts
Stores nationwide
www.joannefabrics.com

A.C. Moore Craft Stores
Stores nationwide
www.acmoore.com

Hobby Lobby
Stores nationwide
www.hobbylobby.com

Michaels Crafts
Stores nationwide
www.michaels.com

Dick Blick Art Supply
www.dickblick.com
Toll free (800) 828-4548
E-mail info@dickblick.com

FLAX Art and Design
www.flaxart.com
Toll free (888) FLAXART (352-9278)

Create for Less
www.createforless.com
Toll free (866) 333-4463

Beads and jewelry:

Rings-n-Things
www.rings-things.com
Toll free (800) 366-2156

Fire Mountain Gems and Beads
www.firemtn.com
Toll free (800) 423-2319

General Bead
Genbead@sbcglobal.net
Tel (619) 336-0100

Alpha Supply, Inc. Jewlery and Lapidary Supplies
www.alpha-supply.com
Toll free (800) 257-4211

Soap, candle, and bath supplies:

Lavender Lane
www.lavenderlane.com
Toll free (888) 593-4400
E-mail healthychoices@lavenderlane.com

LorAnn Oils, Inc
www.lorannoils.com
Toll free (888) 4LORANN (456-7266)

Sweet Cakes Soapmaking Supplies
www.sweetcakes.com
Tel (973) 838-5200

Majestic Mountain Sage
www.thesage.com
Tel (435) 755-0863
E-mail research@the-sage.com

Bramble Berry, Inc.
www.brambleberry.com
Tel (360) 734-8278

Sunburst Bottle Company
www.sunburstbottle.com
Tel (916) 348-5576
E-mail info@sunburstbottle.com

Specialty manufacturers:

Plaid Enterprises Inc:
Paints, glues, the all-wondrous Mod Podge®,
and other craft supplies.
www.plaidonline.com
Toll free (800) 842-4197
E-mail: talk@plaidonline.com

Delta Technical Coatings Inc:
Acrylic paint, varnishes, sealers, and other craft
supplies.
www.deltacrafts.com
Toll free (800) 423-4135
E-mail: advisor@deltacrafts.com

Aleene's and Duncan Crafts
www.aleenes.com
Toll free (800) 438-6226
E-mail: aleenes@duncanmail.com

M&J Trimming:
Fabric trims, fringes, beading, and purse parts.
www.mjtrim.com
Tel (212) 842-5050
E-mail: mjtrim.info@mjtrim.com

Other cool stuff:

American Science & Surplus:
All kinds of random stuff including bottles
and toys.
www.sciplus.com
Tel (847) 982-0870
E-mail: info@sciplus.com

Dollar Fabric.com:
Cheap fabric by the yard.
www.dollarfabric.com
Tel (877) 581-9744
E-mail: admin@dollarfabric.com

Oriental Trading Company, Inc.:
Random toys, craft supplies, and novelties.
www.orientaltrading.com
Toll free (800) 875-8480

Papers by Catherine:
Handmade and decorative paper.
www.papersbycatherine.com
Tel (713) 723-3334
E-email: info@papersbycatherine.com

Lee Valley Tools:
Clockworks and other tools.
www.leevalley.com
Toll free (800) 267-8735
E-mail: customerservice@leevalley.com

Pearl River Department Stores:
Large New York City Chinatown department
store with lots of papers, sandals, and all kinds of
other stuff.
www.pearlriver.com
Toll free (800) 878-2446
E-mail: info@pearlriver.com

General D.I.Y. info sites:

www.hgtv.com
www.diynet.com
www.about.com